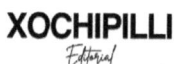

The Bandit as the Origin
of the Mexican Corrido
History and Evolution until our time

Pedro Pablo Marín

The Bandit as the Origin of the Mexican Corrido

First English Edition, Chicago, Illinois, May, 2023.

© Pedro Pablo Marín

© XOCHIPILLI EDITORIAL

Speaking of the Mexican Corrido...

Could it be a coincidence that the protagonists of the *Mexican Corrido* are full of characters who tend to be outside the law? Why in the *Mexican Corrido* Are we fascinated by the figure of the bandit and the drug trafficker as heroes who come from the people? Is this related to a memory of our ancestors who suffered situations of injustice before, during and after the *Mexican Revolution* and did they find their defenders in these characters?

Index

The Mexican Corrido in the Mexican Revolution

The Corrido and its relationship with the epic

Four possible origins of the Corrido

Regionalist origin of the Corrido

The Corrido in the Northeast regions
and Northwestern Mexico

Replacement of the Bandit by the figure of the Narco

The commercial boom of the Corridos:
Chalino Sánchez

The birth of the Corrido Tumbado

Introduction

It is not new that there is currently a growth and a global affinity to *Mexican Corrido*. With the appearance of the musical phenomenon called *Peso Pluma* the Mexican corrido took the place that it had been cherishing for decades with the notable increase in artists, fusions and musical reinventions among which the *Corrido Tumbado* however, the history and evolution of the corrido to the present day is extensive and complex, so one of the intentions of this writing is to add a theoretical effort to the global rise of the Corrido in 2023 and present a general approach to its history and evolution since the time of the Mexican Revolution to our time.

For the majority of Mexicans who live in the north of Mexico, near the border or born in the

United States of Mexican parents, the corrido is something we are born with, it is a music that has always accompanied us and acquires a sign of meeting, party, familiarity and it is precisely this closeness that sometimes does not allow us to know or question its origin and its evolution, it is simply a music that is enjoyed with the family and it matters little to wonder about the deep relationship it has with the history of our families. In this sense, the researcher *Guillermo Hernandez* in his essay *"What Is a Corrido?"*, mentions the following:

"Corridos have been sung for almost two hundred years, yet the genre has tended to remain distant or misunderstood to outsiders of this important ballad tradition of Mexico and the United States" (Hernández).

This misunderstanding about corridos arises from ignorance of the practical function they had during the times of the revolution, that is, that the way in which older generations heard and felt them is very different from that of now, however they continue to maintain an element that has not been lost and is still valid in our time: narrating the exploits of the heroes of the region.

In this text we are going to review how in its origins the corrido was the way of narrating and singing local events, something like a sung news that was transmitted verbally through the towns and *rancherías* since the general population had no other option way to find out about events in other regions.

We will review how the corridos were historical versions that were transmitted musically through which a large part of the population learned about certain events in their community, "corridos have flourished in relative isolation, preserving the views of marginal communities; that is, corridos convey unofficial versions of history" (Hernández). Through performers and composers nomads, these musical pieces fed the spirit of the people as they narrated the exploits of characters who showed signs of bravery when facing the authorities to defend their lands, honor and manhood.

At the level of formal definitions, we will review several investigations that place the origin of the Mexican Corrido in three phases and we will take a tour of the definitions based on its formal musical structure, in this sense we explore its possible origins and we will trace a route of approach to understand the way in which this musical genre was developed from the social and cultural changes located in the northeastern and northwest regions of Mexico and its border with the United States.

To conclude this approach, we will review the proposal that highlights the Regional origin of the Mexican Corrido postulated by the researcher Antonieta Carracedo since due to its narrative nature, the corrido functioned as a form of journalism or transmission of regional news, functioning as a version of the story radically separated from the official version of the government in power. This particular form of journalism highlighted the victories, bravery and exploits of these characters who were labeled by the government as bandits[1] and somehow the displays of courage on the part of these local characters, managed to express the people's desire for justice as a result of the abuses and found a strong resonance, which made this genre a vital chronicle of the liberation aspirations of the communities.

The Mexican Corrido in the Mexican Revolution

We must not forget that one of the founding motives of the uprising in arms that evolved into what we know as the Mexican Revolution was the state of decomposition that existed between the federal government, the rich and the people in general, a relationship of abuse that came becoming

---

[1] The word *bandit* comes from Italian *bandito* , "outside the law", from Vulgar Latin *baniere* , "to proclaim or proscribe", through a Germanic root that it shares with *ban*.

more and more accentuated and that he would find in Porfirio Díaz the symbol par excellence of tyranny. Characters such as Madero, Villa or Zapata became revolutionary and rebellious figures that the people followed with the sole objective of finding a solution to the situation of poverty and one way to highlight and adhere to their achievements was through corridistic compositions:

"Composed, transmitted, and consumed by rural and urban working-classes, people distant from circles of power and prestige, the genre expresses viewpoints that often contradict or stand in direct opposition to dominant perspectives" (Hernández).

The stories told in the corridos evolved into a narrative genre that reported on events of a historical and local nature through colloquial language "Local community issues provided the basic subject matter that inspired corrido composers" local community provided the basic theme that inspired corrido composers."

(Hernández). According to Guillermo Hernández, historian and specialist in the evolution of the corrido, this musical style would be almost two hundred years old, during which time it has found a series of evolutions that are identified in three phases:

- The first phase is linked to the oral transmission of events and this was distributed through songbooks or pamphlets. (Pre Revolution).
- The second phase corresponds to the formal inauguration of corridos analysis in the 1930s and where the intellectual bases for the study of the genre were established.
- The third phase corresponds to the monitoring and contemporary analysis, where a broader and more representative corridistic corpus of the genre was strengthened.

In this sense, the second phase is the most important for the genre because it is here where the first official definition of the corrido arises made by Armando Duvalier "[an] epic-lyric poem, ranging between twenty and thirty octosyllabic quatrains and subject to six basic primary formulas" "[an] epic-lyric poem, of between twenty and thirty eight-syllable quatrains and subject to six basic primary formulas" (Hernández). This definition will be accompanied by a formal structure with which the corrido is narratively organized:

"According to Duvalier, the primary formulas that shape the overall narrative structure of the poem are: (1) Singer's initial address to the audience (2) Place, time, and name of the main character (3) Antecedents to the arguments of the main character (4) Message (5) Main character's farewell (6) Composer's farewell" (Hernádez).

This narrative structure[2] It is related to a way of orderly recounting a historical event, with the main objective of singing the drama and tragedy of a character considered by the people as an example or a hero.

The Corrido and its relationship with the epic

The direct relationship of the corrido with the epic[3], is given from its protagonist. The corrido tends to be epic because it talks about the feats performed by a specific character. "Since the revolutionary and post-revolutionary era, people have also used the corrido as a popular expression or anthem of identity and values represented in the Mexican rebel heroes. " (Badillo). From here comes the importance of the rebellious character, who develops feats and risks his life to defend the values that the people share and from this relationship with

---

[2] Listen to the *Corrido by Emiliano Zapata* as an example of this structure.

[3] Literary genre made up of stories of the exploits of heroes who represent the ideals of a warrior or aristocratic class and of an entire society that associates these people with their origins and destiny as a people.

the epic also comes its dramatic, emotional and violent tone.

Another definition that is worth mentioning is the one collected by Antonio Avitia based on the one that Celedonio Serrano dictates in his work *Corrido Histórico Mexicano* "The corrido is an epic-lyric-tragic genre, [...] it includes all the genres [...] which tells in a simple and straightforward way, all those events that deeply impressed the sensitivity of the people" (Badillo). This definition highlights tragedy as a representative element of the corrido, since these rebel heroes were generally persecuted for defending their rights or were killed by elements of the government. This tragic sensitivity responds precisely to the fact that the corrido, in the vast majority of cases, includes in the narratives of the revolutionary heroes, the ideals, the hopes, the thirst for revenge, for the restitution of property and lands that the people desire.

Another definition of the corrido is that made by Vicente Mendoza "An epic-lyric-narrative genre--with quatrains of variable rhyme [...] that describes events that cause a profound impact on the masses." (Hernández). These definitions coincide mainly in identifying it as an epic-lyrical poem linked to the desire to free oneself from abuse and the thirst for victory. However, these definitions, although they coincide in many of their points, led to more doubts about the origin of the corrido and caused the increase in subsequent research developing new theoretical paths that related the origin of the corrido to other musical styles.

Four possible origins of the Corrido

The studies and definitions surrounding the corrido caused controversy when establishing its definitive origin, which caused an increase in historical and social considerations that were documented. In this desire to establish the origin, the second phase inaugurated in 1930, caused the emergence of theories directly related to historical processes and musical adaptations that already existed previously, in this sense Avitia Hernández proposes four most popular origins of the corrido:

1: "First, it is believed that the origin may be Iberian [...] derived from the Spanish ballads that were imported to America several centuries ago.
2: The second suggests that it comes from the event of colonization itself or its process.
3: The third points to an effect of cultural mixing after colonization.
4: The fourth is the regionalist one, which best describes the Mexican corrido, although it contradicts the previous ones" (Badillo).

Regarding the Iberian origin, researcher Vicente Mendoza mentions that the form of composition of the corrido is similar to that of the Spanish ballads, establishing it as "quartets of variable and assonant rhyme in even verses and is based on "a musical phrase" (Badillo), in turn

Gabriel Delgado López says that "the corrido adopts the epic of traditional Spanish romance (as a metric combination)" (Badillo). In some way, both researchers aim to establish the reference to the Spanish romance novel due to its technical and stylistic composition. Continuing with this definition, the Royal Spanish Academy adheres to the version of Iberian origin, defining the corrido as "a joyful romance in which events from a licentious life are told" (Badillo). Definition that caused discontent since the centrality of these compositions is forgotten: the direct transmission of news within the community and the narration of the exploits of some town character.

In relation to the second origin, researcher Thomas Stanford defends that the corrido had its origin in the colonial era "according to this new approach, the corrido would have emerged in the colonial era, since there is a similarity with the jácara" (Badillo), the *jacaras* they were small musical compositions that told about stories of ruffians or evildoers in a fictional sense.

In this same line and related to the third origin that points to a miscegenation or fusion of genres and definitions, researcher Delgado López mentions that "the term corrido could also be derived from *courante* french due to the similar style of its characteristic music" (Badillo). This comparison is more related to a metric and dance structure, since the *courante* it was sung and danced so quickly that it seemed as if the dancers and performers were running, hence the alleged similarity.

For these reasons and similarities it has become very difficult to determine the origin of the corrido, concludes Avitia.

Regionalist origin of the Corrido

The first three positions that we have just reviewed have their origin in the comparison of musical style, but they fail to consider the region, injustice and the collective, as characteristic elements of the compositions.

As we have already mentioned, the corrido maintains a close relationship with the sensitivity of the town, being the form of communication of news and versions of history that occurred in other towns which formed a sense of solidarity and a way of understanding each other collectively. Since ideals, dreams, desires and aspirations were also shared through the corridos, this consideration will be the heart of Antonieta Carracedo's proposal regarding the origin of the corrido.

Antonieta Carracedo, provided one of the most decisive definitions that we have of the Mexican corrido since in her definition she radically discards the relationship that was intended to be established between the *Spanish Romancero*, the *Jácara* colonial and the *Courante* french, comparisons sustained only in their stylistic relationship.

The researcher mentions that both the Spanish romance, the jácara and the courante had a fictional character and did not consider real historical events that came from the sensitivity of the people as the foundations of their composition, unlike the corrido that keeps the collective meaning of a real event such as fundamental support of its creation and assuming the variants depending on the region of origin "Tragedy, verses, ball, mornings, corrido, dance, narration, history, memories. The content of the letter may change depending on the region or state where it is written." (Badillo). In this direction, Badillo cites the work of González Moreno arguing that the origin of the corrido can be traced directly as a:

"Traveling school of history, rescuing the hidden echoes in the haciendas, in the stripe stores; there where the whip and misery most deeply wounded the imagination of the people. It was the art of the anonymous mass, democracy sung by those below, of those who had no money but a lot of courage" (Badillo).

This regionalist position gives us a better clue when it comes to tracing the origin of the corrido and its evolution to our time, since as we have mentioned, the stories told in the corridos have a close relationship with the specific region where they take place. They compose, sing and are distributed.

In this sense, emphasizing the regional aspect proposed by Carracedo, researcher José Cuello says that what is known as regionalism is created when "the historical experience of a population that defines a geographic area as a region by granting it certain demographic characteristics, political and cultural" (Castro), this definition of region is directly linked to what Carracedo postulates as the origin of corridos in that it is from the historical and cultural experience of a population that musical compositions come from.

In this way, the revolutionary bandit gained cultural and social value in certain regions because of his interest in the well-being of specific people who lived in the agricultural, mining and hacienda sectors, causing admiration for them, since in the midst of chaos of the government's abuses at that time, these characters lived outside the law, causing great headaches for the authorities and earning the sympathy of the people, who somehow saw in their exploits a form of revenge, having as their greatest popular example of these bandits to General Pancho Villa.

The regionalist origin refers us mainly to the social context in which this genre became a system of narrative communication of the events that occurred within the town and portrayed the enmity towards the government, an enmity that detonated in the revolutionary struggle but that It had been creeping in since long before the Revolution:

"Towards 1867, with the execution of Emperor Maximilian [...] with the defeat of the external enemies of the liberal republic in Mexico [...] the successive governments of liberalism [...] oriented their military efforts towards the elimination of its main internal enemies: bandits, peasant movements and/or indigenous uprisings" (Parra).

The so-called bandits began to gain popularity in the context after the independence of Mexico given the poor economic situation of the country and especially due to the precariousness of the merchandise transportation system that somehow facilitated the operation of groups of bandits. Later it would be these same groups of bandits who would join the revolutionary cause since they were previously subjected to the same persecution applied to the peasants, through which they were dispossessed of their lands:

"In the last third of the 19th century, banditry was subjected to the same vigorous official provision of crushing and extermination applied to peasant communities that opposed with arms the confiscation of their lands by government agents or by private interests" (Parra).

This dynamic and system of persecution by the State towards groups of bandits, peasants and indigenous people extended until reaching the period of General Porfirio Díaz where the relationship was already more than damaged and the spirits of a crushed people had reached their limit. However, abuses of authority and government measures worsened:

"In the enlightened dictatorship of General Porfirio Díaz (1876-1911), he reinforced the Rural Corps, a peasant police organization, whose mission, quite successful, was to pursue and eliminate highwaymen [...] and pacify to the Mexican countryside" (Parra).

The so-called *Rural's* they were also in charge of looking after the interests of the landowners, landowners and miners, trying in turn to prevent these groups of bandits from giving some protection to the people of the countryside as a defense against the abuses of private interests and the Díaz government. .

According to studies, the first corridos were composed from the time before Porfirio Díaz but it was in the chaos of the Revolution where they became popular and the figure of the bandit brought about the more or less massive production of corridos.

One of the first recorded corridos that narrate the actions of the bandit is the one that includes the story of "Leonardo Rivera, who died in 1841 during the time of Santa Anna, who was a local leader and dedicated himself to banditry in Nuevo León, perhaps from a conflict between federalists and centralists" (González). From the appearance of this corrido, corridos based on figures of bandits began to appear consecutively, such as "Heraclio Bernal (1885), Ignacio Parra (1892), Reyes Ruiz (1893), Demetrio Jauregui (1896) [...] Likewise, the corridos of Joaquín Murrieta (1853) may be added, whose corridos are still very popular in the border area of Mexico and the United States" (González). These corridos belong to the time before the revolution, which shows their direct relationship with the outlaw character, resulting in the great spread of the corrido since each region had its own defending heroes, as Antonieta Carracedo maintains, "The content of the lyrics may change depending on the region or state where it is written." (Badillo). In this sense, we know that the bandit is always a character deeply affiliated with his region and is honored by the local people; The thirst for justice of a people wounded by abuse found in the groups of bandits the leaders who waged war against landowners and rural people, finding in this music the resonance of a justice that was denied to them.

In this context, the bandit begins to take on the character of a hero, defender of the people, demonstrating bravery and giving his life (from which it acquires its tragic epic character) when sustaining a violent struggle against the government forces and which we find narrated in the origin. of the corridos "It is a protest that has nothing to do with abolishing exploitation, but rather with the injustice and despotism of authorities and officials" (González). Under this circumstance, the figure of the bandit was used by the Mexican elite to justify their dominance over the lower classes, while the Anglo-Saxon communities used it to reaffirm their superiority over the rural people. "Although his fictional image sometimes reproduced the romantic type of European literature, most often the image of the Mexican bandit was imagined as a metaphor of degraded masculinity and backwardness" (Parra). In this sense, the narrative of the corrido not only collects the collective feeling in its stories, but also inaugurates the figure of the truly Mexican bandit, a heroic figure whose origins lie in the historical events of the time "we must remember that the hero epic represents values of the community and corresponds more to moments of crisis such as will happen in the period of the Revolution" (González), and it is precisely in the figure of the bandit based on real and collective conflicts from which it emerges in the most faithful and authentic Mexican Corrido.

For many researchers, it is within the margins of this brief context where the regionalist origin of the corrido can be sustained. This origin makes sense when we consider the particularity of the historical events in Mexican politics and the social situation of the people who were struggling between death and injustice, highlighting the sense of collectivity to which already existing metric forms such as the of Spanish romance, but it was not the other way around.

Therefore, the bandit's activity before and in the midst of revolutionary chaos, linked to specific regions and a desire for collective justice, awakens the need to position them as heroes who alleviate the suffering inflicted by the authorities in power, probably in this sense. The Mexican corrido is still valid since it provides a cathartic sense in the face of injustice and abuse, but in which regions of the country was it where the corrido reached its greatest importance? Who or who are the direct heirs of the revolutionary bandit and who resumed the role of heroes and defenders of the people?

The Corrido in the Northeast and Northwest regions of Mexico

As far as the Mexican corrido is concerned, the region is of utmost importance, since the rise of the corrido occurs in the region known as northeastern Mexico, where the greatest exponents emerged and were consolidated from the 1940s onwards. and although the regional aspect is important, it must be understood that a given region not only has to do with the geographical boundary between states, but that the region shares and is founded on a collective consciousness regarding social phenomena and they share a sensitivity and way to see life.

It is no coincidence that in the northeast of Mexico the corrido has its maximum splendor, since in this region there were already musical expressions such as *chotis, redova and polka* inherited from the Czechoslovak, German and Polish migrations in the regions of Nuevo León and Tamaulipas and that when merged with the corrido established in the revolution, gave birth to what was called Corrido Norteño, this was largely due to the instruments used to interpret a *polka* for example, such as the accordion, bass sixth and double bass coincided perfectly when composing and performing a corrido.

In this sense, researcher Manuel Ceballos gives us the following definition about the Mexican northeast: "A geopolitical and geoeconomic space located at the confluence of the four states that make up the Mexican northeast: Tamaulipas, Nuevo León, Coahuila and Texas. (This unit implies) complexity to understand the interrelationship of the cities and subregions included in it" (Castro). This definition is important for our analysis since the corrido was strongly consolidated in this region, becoming identified as northern or ranchera music.

On the other hand, starting in the 1940s with the increase in migration from Mexico to the United States, the northeastern region took center stage since a large part of the corridistic compositions of this time reflected the desire to return to the homeland and the desire to escape poverty, manifestations that were not only expressed in literature but also in bullfights.

"A determining element was the Braceros program. It was implemented from 1942 to 1964 during World War II. Mexican farmers and workers moved to the United States in search of economic improvement. They represented cheap labor in farming activities or in the construction of railways. Norteño music increased its popularity in that period. The songs portrayed the daily life, the experiences of their transfer, beliefs and attitudes of the migrants" (Castro).

At this time, the growth of the northern corrido was closely linked to the construction of the northeastern regions based on social, cultural and political phenomena that were narrated musically and shaped the identity and consciousness of the northern population, highlighting bravery, the frontier, the desire for progress and the bond with the land and women.

This collective consciousness found its main exponents from 1940 and 1950 with *Los alegres de*

Terán who led the northern corrido at that time, in 1960 *Carlos and José* they established variations regarding the themes and by the 1970s, *Los Cadetes de Linares,* one of the most important northeastern corrido groups, they took center stage with their northern corridos that talked about ranch life, love tragedies, revenge, and the exploits of bandits on the border with the United States.

In this sense, the corrido norteño dominated the entire northeastern region for decades, but by the 1980s onwards, a group originating from the region of *Mocorito, Sinaloa,* called *Los Tigres del Norte* they established themselves as the greatest exponents of the genre, positioning the northwest region of Mexico in the main corrido production area.

This transfer from the northeastern corrido to the northwestern corrido was directly influenced by smuggling, since in those years Sinaloa was the region identified as a reference for smuggling at the national level and although in the period before the revolution the bandit rebelled against the government and in the revolution took entire towns by force, after the revolution the bandit was going to traffic drugs and the musicians were going to place this criminal activity in the composition of their corridos as a means to get out of poverty, highlighting social inequality and lack of opportunities as has been maintained since the revolutionary era.

In this sense, the corrido genre has adapted to the social and political conditions of Mexico over the years and has strengthened sympathy for figures who openly demonstrate against the government.

Replacement of the Bandit by the figure of the Narco

As we have been analyzing, the origin of the corrido has had a series of recognition patterns and it seems that the regionalist origin is the one that best adapts to the circumstances and the musical testimonies that we can hear today, especially because the figure of the bandit or the outlaw character, only considering the social, cultural and political evolution in Mexico, this figure has evolved until it leads to the character of the Drug Trafficker.

The origin of smuggling developed on the Mexico-United States border was culturally characterized by giving rise to musical expressions that explicitly spoke of drug smuggling. "The border between Mexico and the United States would witness countless clandestine transactions. Smugglers were defined as adventurous men who jumped over fences seduced by the feat" (Dávila). In this sense, the feat, mockery and victory against the enemy begins to be celebrated in the bullfights at a massive level. This celebration, as we analyzed when reviewing the regionalist origin, maintained its direct relationship with real events that served as a narrative history that informed the population of the achievements of its heroes "the majority of the corridos of the 1930s of the 20th century have a solid basis in real events and reflect the evolution of drug smuggling. As you can see, the corridos "Por morfína y cocaína" and "El contrabandista", both recorded in 1934" (Dávila). In these compositions the figure of the "generous bandit" who helped the poor with the profits obtained from smuggling began to appear.

Another important factor in monitoring the evolution of the corrido will be related to the specific areas of marijuana and poppy cultivation, being the region of *Badiraguato* the main area where this activity was carried out "Badiraguato, Sinaloa, became an important drug producing center and epicenter of distribution to the United States. [...] Badiraguato became an emblem of drug trafficking" (Dávila). Smuggling became a means to escape poverty, oppression and hunger inherited from revolutionary times, mainly by inhabitants of the mountains who suffered extreme conditions of poverty but who had a high level of knowledge in poppy cultivation and saw a exit to its condition by cultivating it.

Until this moment, the historical route of the corrido had maintained its production at a regional level, but all that changed in the 1970s, the year in which a corrido dedicated to smuggling was recorded for the first time in its history. "In the seventies, it was the moment of the narcocorridos boom. The first trafficker bullfights were officially registered in the Society of Authors and Composers of Mexico" (Dávila). And just as had happened decades ago in the revolutionary era, the government began to deploy operations dedicated to dismantling those organizations and according to the records of the time, these operations occurred most crudely in the Sierra de*Badiraguato* causing a displacement of people towards *Culiacan* the capital of *Sinaloa* carrying with them their cultural baggage in relation to drugs and music "The abandonment of the mountains and their transfer to the state capital generated social maladjustment, led to unemployment, more violence and the increase in drug addiction in Culiacán [...] Also, the presence of musicians who played accordion and bass Segundo increased" (Dávila). Just at that time of tension between the government and smuggling was when the first national corridos were announced by *Los Tigres del Norte*, run like *La Banda del Carro Rojo*, *Una camioneta gris* and *Contrabando y Tarición*, they narrated the reality that had been developing for decades and found their greatest success among the public.

The commercial boom of corridos: Chalino Sánchez

Although in its origins the transmission of the corrido was from town to town by nomadic singers out loud, with the advancement of technology the corrido experienced one of its most significant changes in terms of its distribution, influence and popularity.

The growth of the recording industry, the notable growth of smuggling, Mexican migration to the United States and the desire to narrate and consume stories associated with this cultural boom focused on the figure of *Chalino Sánchez,* Sinaloan singer who promoted the corrido revolution.

A determining element in the massification of the corrido was the recording industry, which led to notable growth, beginning to shape what is now known as the music industry *Narcocorrido*, music that was widely consumed both in Mexico and by immigrants in the United States "In the nineties the recording industry promoted the production, recording and dissemination of the narcocorrido [...] This, because it was a very popular musical genre in a Spanish-speaking audience, which developed simultaneously on both sides of the border between Mexico and the United States" (Dávila). And it is precisely in this historical and social framework, where it appeared *Chalino Sánchez,* one of the greatest exponents of the genre of *Narcocorrido*, something like a bandit *superstar* that revolutionized the industry by establishing the foundations for the corrido to sink its roots deep into the public's taste, *Chalino* it told real stories but introduced the variant of the corrido on request, now people who had been financially successful had the luxury of requesting a composition of their achievements:

"Sometimes it is perceived that some ordinary men, with a certain economic capacity and a certain detachment from life, seek to be part of this mythical sphere that the corridos have formed, although in the concrete world they do not belong to it. They "order" them: they ask the corridista to incorporate them into that fictional world, which, without a doubt, is already influencing that other one, the concrete one" (Osorio).

In this way, the collective meaning of the corrido became individualized by focusing on personal history, but the values of progress, improvement and courage shared by this entire region continued to be praised. On the other hand, the rise of the narcocorrido that inaugurated *Chalino Sánchez* it was not only on a musical level, but it inaugurated an entire cultural movement called "*El Chalinazo*" which included style of dress, language, musical taste and specific ways of making a living "young city dwellers adopted that northern way of dressing that was close to the Mexican ranchero, a drug dealer appearance *chic*. The style was characterized by the use of hats, jeans, showy silk shirts, jackets and cowboy boots made of exotic animal skin, large buckles and gold chains" (Dávila). This cultural revolution linked to drug trafficking and corrido continued its course, establishing itself on both sides of the border and soon other musical influences such as *Gangsta Rap* mainly promulgated by Chicano youth, they were finding a place within the sound and lyrics of what was popularly associated with the corrido and they also had their own heroes who moved underground, later when the *Gangsta Rap* lost its sense of being outside the law at the end of the 20th century, the *Trap* by the hand of *Lil Wayne* at the beginning of the 21st century as a new form of clandestinity in the field of urban youth and it is precisely here where the new generations in both Mexico and the United States adopted these influences and would begin to form the bases and musical evolution that would bring the birth of what we now know as the *Corrido Tumbado*.

The birth of the Corrido Tumbado

As we observed up to this point, the *Mexican Corrido* has maintained an internal movement deeply linked to the spirit of each time, this in some way informs us that the conditions of inequality, injustice and poverty have been maintained over time since the difference between the motivations for action of the bandit and the of the drug trade, however, the young heirs of this movement already in some way enjoy the fruits of years of socio-political and economic transformations and already have access to a global culture that will significantly influence the evolution and compositions of their corridos.

Currently, the corrido has taken on a new air and a new style, causing a new revolution that can well be compared *Chalinazo* of the nineties in regard to a cultural and musical revolution among youth, also provoking strong criticism for its relationship with criminal associations, even censoring some corridos, such as the corrido *"Cuerno Azulado"* by Natanael Cano is prohibited in some states of Mexico, however, as we have been observing in this text, it seems that history is only repeating itself in a circle, because the main motivation that arises before, during and after the revolution has been the same: praising feats of outlaw characters.

Let's say that the corrido has only been updated according to the evolution of the industry, technology, and new musical and cultural expressions, but the heart of the corrido was and continues to be telling the stories related to the feelings of the people and their relationship of sympathy with the bandit.

In this sense, if already at the time of *Los Tigres del Norte* and of *Chalino* the public learned that "the modern hero has replaced the horse and the gun with the *cheyene* of the year and the goat's horn" (Simonett). Under this context, a young man *Hermosillo, Sonora* (northwest) called *Nathanael Cano* will change the course of the corrido since he is the heir to three musical influences such as *Narcocorrido* represented in *Chalino*, he *Gangsta Rap* of Chicano youth and *Trap* inaugurated by Lil Wayne mediated by globalization, he will find the need to make a new form of corrido linked to a youth that no longer identifies with boots and hats but with high fashion *Balenciaga* and *Gucci*, who no longer identifies with horses but with sports cars, who no longer identifies with being an immigrant but rather has both nationalities or a visa and who no longer identifies with traditional and rural values but lives immersed in a globalized world.

This new way of making corridos represented by urban youth is very far from having the rural experience and this is noticeable in the lyrics of their songs. You can even see that the compositions are in first person, that is, they narrate their own exploits and their experiences. achievements, putting themselves as characters in their corridos, this is a direct inheritance from hip hop and trap:

"The word "trap" has become a common prefix for hip hop-influenced subgenres, even if they do not share the qualities of trap music, which is characterized by sharp snares; booming bass; and hazy, minor-key melodies. Trapcorridos are primarily composed and performed by Mexican Americans around urban themes or personalities" (Fernández).

This new movement led by artists such as *Nathanael Cano, Fuerza Regida, Peso Pluma* and *Junior H*, has left the regional and is now known worldwide as *Corrido Tumbado*.

Currently the highest representative of *Corrido Tumbado* is the singer called *Peso Pluma* (Hassan Emilio Kabande Laija) who has broken language barriers and appeared for the first time on national television in the United States on the program *Jimmy Fallon*, also holds participation in the festival *Coachella*, winner of a *Grammy* and that broke the reproduction records on all platforms worldwide, surpassing Latin artists such as *Bad Bunny* and *Shakira* and above all, it has brought the Spanish language to musical contexts where English is predominant. This singer continues a tradition of praising certain drug trafficking figures and criminal associations such as *Cartel of Sinaloa* and makes direct allusions to *Chapo Guzman* with which it is not far from the corridistic tradition inherited from the regionalist connection of the Mexican corrido even though its musical impact is already worldwide.

The truth is that we went from a collective sense to a more individualistic sense associated with the times, but that does not mean that the collective sense of the corrido has been lost. In the lyrics of this new expression, the figure of the bandit continues to be the central axis. of the stories narrated maintaining the epic sense of pride, violence and victory corresponding to its regionalist origin.

The great boom of this genre currently also reveals the taste of a young and heterogeneous audience that already transcends the limits of the region "The corrido style of song is prosperous not only in Mexico, particularly in rural areas, but also in large urban centers of the United States, such as Los Angeles, Detroit and Chicago" (Simonett), and this confirms the reality of a globalized world that has led to a greater reach of Mexican regional music.

There is no doubt that we are facing the popularity of the corrido beyond the borders of the region and possibly it is due to the mythical and even religious character with which bandits and drug lords are exalted and considered. The bandit as a kind of antihero exists in the narrative and epic versions of every corner of the planet and the current massification of the corrido and the regional Mexican notably reflects its link to a narrative tradition in regards to the development of characters who remain outside the law and who usually emerge from the oppressed class.

As Mexicans, it is very possible that our families have consumed the corrido as a form of news and in some way saw themselves represented at the time by these characters. In this sense, throughout this historical journey we have been able to understand a little more about the evolution of this musical genre linked to popular taste and in some way locate and understand the internal mechanisms related to its current popularity.

He *Mexican Corrido* it will continue to evolve as the generations advance, since it is a music that follows the evolution of culture, of the times and remains deeply linked to the feelings of the people and their desires.

References

Badillo, José Adrián. "From the corrido to the narcocorrido: some aspects of the evolution and cultural effects of the mythification and apotheosis of narcotics trafficking in popular Mexican sung poetry."*Aula lirica 7 Magazine on Iberian and Ibero-American poetry*, 2015.

Parra, Max. "Pancho Villa and the bullfight of the revolution."*Caravelle (1988-), June 2007, No. 88, Chanter le bandit. Ballads and laments from Latin America* (June 2007), pp. 139-1 University of California , 2007 .

González, Aurelio. "The character of the "social" (social?) bandit in the corrido.*School of Mexico*, 2015.

Hernández, Guillermo E. "What Is a Corrido? Thematic Representation and Narrative Discourse". *Studies in Latin American Popular Culture*, vol. 18, Jan. 1999, p. 69.

Dávila, C. J. B. Burgos, C. (in press). "Narcocorridos: Background of the bullfight tradition and drug trafficking in Mexico."*Studies in Latin American Popular Culture.*

Lobato Osorio, L. (2003). "Chalino Sánchez: character corridos."*Magazine of Popular Literatures.* Year III/number 1, January-June 2003. Mexico: Faculty of Philosophy and Letters, National Autonomous University of Mexico.

Simonett, H. (2004). "Musical subculture: the commercial narcocorrido and the commissioned narcocorrido."*Caravelle (1988-)*, 179-193.

Fernández, C. (2021). "Corridos: (Mostly) True Stories in Verse with Music". *Journal of Folklore and Education*, 8.

www.ingramcontent.com/pod-product-compliance
Lightning Source LLC
Chambersburg PA
CBHW030511220526
45464CB00006B/2752